W9-AAJ-799

MOTHERS

AND

DAUGHTERS

Also by June Cotner

Animal Blessings
Baby Blessings
Bedside Prayers
Bless the Day
Comfort Prayers
Dog Blessings
Family Celebrations
Forever in Love
Get Well Wishes
Graces
Heal Your Soul, Heal the World
House Blessings
Looking for God in All the Right Places
Miracles of Motherhood
Say A Little Prayer
Serenity Prayers
The Home Design Handbook
To Have and to Hold
Wedding Blessings

MOTHERS

AND

DAUGHTERS

A Poetry Celebration

JUNE COTNER

HARMONY BOOKS · NEW YORK

Copyright © 2001 by June Cotner

All rights reserved. Published in the United States by Harmony Books,
an imprint of the Crown Publishing Group, a division of Random House LLC,
a Penguin Random House Company, New York.

www.crownpublishing.com

Harmony Books is a registered trademark, and the Circle colophon
is a trademark of Random House LLC.

Originally published in the United States by Harmony Books,
New York, in 2001.

Design by JoAnne Metsch

Library of Congress Cataloging-in-Publication Data

Mothers and daughters: a poetry celebration / [selected] by June Cotner.
Includes index.
1. Mothers and daughters—Poetry 2. American Poetry—20th century.
3. Mothers—Poetry. I. Cotner, June, 1950—
PS595.M65 M68 2001
811'.50803520431—dc21   00-063282

ISBN 978-0-385-36476-8

Printed in the United States of America

1 3 5 7 9 8 6 4 2

2015 Sterling Proprietary Edition

This book is dedicated with much love and appreciation to

my mother,
BETTY ELVIRA BAXTER
(1925–1961)

my daughter,
KIRSTEN COTNER MYRVANG

and a dear woman who treated me like her own daughter,
JANIE TUCKER STUART
(1924–1992)

Acknowledgments

MY MOST loving "thank you" is due to my own mother, Betty Elvira Baxter, who died when I was eleven. Through my mother's love, care, and compassion, I'm able to be a better mother to my children, Kyle and Kirsten.

Deepest gratitude goes to my agent, Denise Marcil, who responded with tremendous enthusiasm after reading the manuscript, calling it "a terrific collection." *Mothers and Daughters* is now my ninth published book, and I owe much of my publishing success to Denise.

I'm extremely grateful that Linda Loewenthal at Random House immediately saw the importance of these poems, which express real-life mother-daughter love, and decided it was a perfect book to publish. Through Linda's careful guidance and suggestions, *Mothers and Daughters* became a stronger book.

Also, I appreciate the attention given to *Mothers and Daughters* by the wonderful staff at Random House: Teryn Johnson and Jeena Lee, associate editors; Liana Faughnan, senior production editor; Linnea Knollmueller, production associate; and Darlene Faster, publicity assistant.

As always, my husband, Jim, is my main anchor and support—providing much love and encouragement, as well as practical help in keeping our household running smoothly. My dear children, Kyle and Kirsten, are a tremendous source of inspiration to me and always share their love so generously in countless ways. They make me forever grateful that I'm their mother.

I'm enormously grateful for my talented assistants in the office: Cheryl Edmonson (book production and overall office management), Rebecca Pirtle (obtaining permissions and coordinating my publicity events), Lacey Menne, Virginia Donald, and Gemma Arcangel (typing, filing, and errands). Others in the local community have extended themselves in the creation of my books. Specifically, the staff at both the Poulsbo and Kingston libraries have obtained a number of reference books for me; Suzanne Droppert, owner of Liberty Bay Books, gives me continual feedback at each stage of a book's production; and Kevin Jennings, computer consultant, brings good cheer my way as he helps me with my sometimes errant computer.

Mothers and Daughters would not be the book it is without the inclusion of outstanding, heartfelt poems from poets who have contributed to my anthologies for many years now. Thank you so much for your treasured words! You should be pleased to know that your poems survived the scrutiny of my review of over 3,000 submissions. Then, after I selected my favorites, my "test market" panel gave me their feedback on which poems should be in the book. Specifically, for providing a careful critique, I'd like to thank editors Linda Loewenthal (of Random House) and Joyce Standish (who has her own editing company in Las Vegas, "papers").

I'd like to express deep appreciation to the following poets who lent their expertise to this book and gave me a careful critique: Barbara Crooker (prolific poet who has been published in six of my anthologies, and winner of many poetry awards), Maureen Tolman Flannery (editor of *Knowing Stones: Poems of Exotic Places* and author of *Remembered into Life*), Susan Fridkin (author of *One Woman*, a poetry tribute to her late mother-in-law), Margaret Anne Huffman (award-winning journalist, author of *Through the Valley: Prayers for Violent Times* and twenty-nine other books), Sherri Waas Shunfenthal (author of *Sacred Voices: Women of Genesis Speak*), Donna Wahlert (award-winning poet and contributor to *Heal Your Soul, Heal the World, Animal Blessings,* and this book), and Barbara Younger (author of *Purple Mountain Majesties: The Story of Katharine Lee Bates and "America the Beautiful"*), and her daughter, Katherine A. Younger.

Rounding out the perspective in helping me make the final selections for *Mothers and Daughters,* I'd like to thank the following individuals: Virginia Lynn Bradley, Jennifer Jane Callen, Suzanne Droppert, Cheryl Edmonson, Shawna Erickson, Sue Gitch, Deborah Ham, Alisa Huckell, Patricia Huckell, Laurie McKinley, Lacey Menne, Kirsten Cotner Myrvang, Susan C. Peterson, Elyse Margaret Trevors, and Sandi Van Ausdal.

A special thanks to the fine poets whose poems did not make the final cut, due to page-length limitations. I agonized deeply over making the final selections for this book.

My last thanks to God, who blesses my life with energy and inspiration—helping me become a conduit to share so many beautiful poems.

Contents

7. LEAVING HOME / 95

8. ADULTHOOD / 109

14. INSPIRATION / 185

Mothers

and

Daughters

A Letter to Readers

THE SELECTIONS in this book are a result of years of collecting poems that touched me emotionally because they so accurately reflect my feelings as a mother, daughter, and granddaughter. I saved these precious verses long before I imagined they would become a book. They are very special to me because they link me to my childhood memories of my mother and grandmothers, my memories as a mother (from pregnancy to now), while they also open a view of roads yet to travel with my daughter (and maybe even a future granddaughter!).

Many of us who are mothers already know that being a mother is the toughest job there is. In a single day you can travel from the depths of frustration to the pinnacle of elation! As the years pass and I watch my children mature, I find that I have a more complete understanding and a deeper appreciation of what my own mother and grandmothers have gone through. As mothers, we ensure our immortality with each moment spent with our children. Little moments, over and over, mold our children's foundation, a cache of learning that they will pass on to their children. What an immense responsibility we have. The impact we have on future generations is so cleverly hidden in our daily routines.

Lately, I've been struck by the simplicity of this thought: Good relationships are made up of positive shared experiences, which become cherished memories over time. Something as simple as daily good-morning hugs can become a legacy that will last for generations. One of my goals in compiling *Mothers and Daughters* was to put together a book that would honor and celebrate mothers and daughters—a book that my daughter and I could read together and laugh and cry over as we reminisce about our own lives and treasured memories.

After reading the manuscript for *Mothers and Daughters*, my friend Elyse Trevors said, "This was a very emotional experience and I thoroughly enjoyed every word! These poems inspired me, moved me—to see into the past as well as the future. I came away from your book enlightened and grateful for capturing a glimpse of the potential my daughter and I have as we grow together. Thank you for this wonderful opportunity."

Another friend, Patricia Huckell, commented after reading the manuscript, "I laughed, I cried, I sighed, I sobbed, I tingled as I read *Mothers and Daughters*. This is a fabulous book! It's so wonderful to read something that honors and acknowledges mothers in this way." I find I have many of the same reactions as Patricia, even after innumerable rereadings of the book. I am always struck by the depth and intensity of the poems. I, too, laugh, cry, sigh, sob, and tingle.

As I find myself transitioning from motherhood toward grandmotherhood, and watch my own daughter journey toward motherhood, I can't help but reflect on the special bond we share because of this common road we travel. Moment by moment, interaction by interaction, and experience by experience, we create the foundation that will affect generations yet to come. What an incredible legacy we women share.

1

Pregnancy

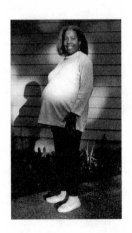

DANCING PARTNERS

I dance in a cumbersome,
out-sized waltz of new life
in love with my body
as it blooms and hovers
over the tiny being
cradled near my heart
as if already on my lap.
I savor outlandish cravings,
rehearsals for a lifetime of yearnings
on behalf of this becoming-daughter.
Naked in morning sunlight,
I anoint my roundness with oil,
lullabying its nestling, who, in
matching conception and gestation
is growing a new me: her mother.

Margaret Anne Huffman

PREGNANT LOVE

I have never been so full—
it spills from my eyes, pushes out from my belly
day by day hour by hour, I am larger.
Though I can never catch that moment
of motion and expansion,
any more than I could witness
the first cells dividing,
or the hands of the great-grandfather clock moving,
the moon arcing across the sky,
or the peony bush starting from green stubs
in my backyard, then flourishing into June
with wild pink happiness.

Andrea Potos

The Conception

Suddenly, you are. In an instant,
a fraction of a nanosecond; somewhere between was not and is,
the not yet and now—you become.

Unaware of your presence; yet you are there.
Silently, without detection,
you come into being and take your place.

You change me; rearrange me, without request.
You mold me into what you need;
my entire being complies.

A part of me, yet your own.
Miraculous metamorphosis within my womb;
that chrysalis of life.

Lost in wonder.
Both blessing and burden are mine, as a piece of eternity
lodges deep within my members.

Part of an eternal plan set in motion.
And I, the chosen vessel, stand in awe;
blessed,
humbled,
undone.

Jill Noblit MacGregor

THE GROWING INTO

Sometimes I'll get a flash:
your grown-up face, your infancy
vanishing like the images
in a flipbook.

In my last trimester,
standing before the full-length
mirror, I thought I could see
your outline through my stretch-
marked skin. Head rounded over,
wrists and ankles crossed, knees
at chest. I could fast forward
your life by thumbing through
a calendar. August, when you'd
be born, next May when
you'd be crawling.

And my own face would age
as I neared term. Every day
more like my mother's. Today
I noticed the fine sandpapery
dots under my eyes and across
my nose, the same ones
now prominent on my mother's face.
I am settling into the outlines
of her eyes, her mouth.

My body will not recover from
pregnancy. These raisin nipples,
bird tracks on my belly, thighs,
tell-tale line from pubis to navel,
and my dark, scarred vulva,
split to the third degree.

Dreaming, I see my mother's
multipara belly, even darker
and softer than my own, bread dough
stretched with each of her three offspring.
In my dream she sends *duk* and *mandoo*
with which I make soup. I wake
with an urgency to call her:
she'd be glad to know
we're eating well.

Peggy Hong

How might I entice you to be born,
little one still cushioned in my womb?
Do you hear the sound of rain
playing against the windows?
We thirst for nothing here.

Downstairs
your sister and father are dancing
to jazz trumpet and drums.
They are doing knock-kneed spins,
waving their fingers, rolling their eyes,
and sticking out their tongues.

Upstairs,
I am dreaming
great bellied, alone.
The bed quilt's a mosaic of
rich reds, greens, and golds.
Voluptuous lilies spill
their heady fragrance throughout the room.
If you could smell them,
you'd feel heaven is here.

Ingrid Goff-Maidoff

WITH CHILD

My life as I always claimed it
is already receding
further and further from me each moment—
just as the stars reached beyond
their original birth
toward the far edges of the universe—
an unstoppable expansion
that is my old life leaving
as the new moves in
to take its place at the center.

Andrea Potos

I WILL WRITE ABOUT YOU AS A MYSTERY

I will write about you as a mystery
with question marks
and blank spaces.

I cannot write about your eyes
or your future.

There are no answers.

I will write about your small kicks inside of me
and the worries you stir in my heart.

I will use words like
friend, gift, stranger.

I will say you are a blank page that still needs to be written.

Your story will be one of promise
with words of joy celebrating
your soul.

Sheila O'Connor

2

Birth

TO MY DAUGHTER

Early
morning I had
planted seeds, cucumber,
melon, squash—I pressed them into
warm earth.

The blood
in my body
sang and I listened for
a cry to join my own—straining
to hear.

And there
you were, all pink,
unfolding in our hands,
a blossom opening with a squall:
daughter.

Ann E. Michael

HEART'S CHILD: IN HONOR OF
MY ADOPTED DAUGHTER

Pink roses I'd fashioned from air
would be no less mysterious
than the new gold and pink daughter,
where once there was none,
who smiles, sleeping, in my arms.

In a wondrous greening of my soul,
I am no longer just me, I am a mother.
Ah, but more than a mere splitting of cells
in the tapestry of a womb, my daughter
and I are chambers in one another's hearts.

Margaret Anne Huffman

FIRST DAUGHTER

This is a bond more tightly sealed,
this sharing the task of childbirth
with an infant who may someday know the same.

Maureen Tolman Flannery

ATTENDING THE BIRTH OF
MY GRANDDAUGHTER

I stood between the O of your mother's panting
mouth and the roundness of her belly.
Your father gripped her hand
at her thigh, bracing her bent knee
as she pushed you through that elastic circle.

We saw the roundness, the top of your head,
now a tiny ear, a chin, soft shoulder,
then your belly and cord and legs and toes
all there at once: ruddy, wiped off, clamped
off, handed off to your mother, your father.

I touched you, round under my hand.

Now I take my turn feeding you
at home on the sofa, under only a midnight moon.
The stripe of light falls across your face
catching your eyes, the O of your mouth,
slender fingers moving in shadow.

I hold you up to the moon
like a shaman, like a grandmother;
I ask for health, wisdom, grace
to encircle your head, tiny ear, chin,
shoulders, belly, legs, toes   forever.

Donna Wahlert

TIDELINE

Your birth came as a storm,
pounded by contractions
so strong, I thought
the walls would break,
but we made it, my starfish,
lying beached and spent
in the clean green room.

Your ears, my dear,
are tiny shells;
you raise your brows
and whole sandbars appear.
Your little crab hands
scuttle and hide.
I run at full tide
with love and milk,
while your quiet face
ripples with dreams
like lacy kelp
in a tidal pool.

Barbara Crooker

BOND

I am enchanted by this blessed mystery—
why you, of all possible infants,
and I, of all possible mothers,
meet here and now to stare with wonder
deeply into one another's eyes.

Maureen Tolman Flannery

PLACENTA PREVIA

Twice the doctors pronounced you dead.
But somehow your cells continued to divide,
forming continents of limbs, peninsulas of ears.

And my body, knowing it could not let you slip,
closed around your fragile formation,
cradled you upon a magenta cushion.

I wondered who you could be, stuck inside
such darkness and would I be lucky enough
to find out? After thirty-seven days of lying

on my back, acting like "a big pink incubator,"
dreaming of showers and espresso and wind,
no one could tell me that you would survive.

When they cut your cocoon open, then pulled
you from me, I stared as they placed an infant
in a clear bassinet under bright lamps—never

could I describe the relief. I did not know
this was the easiest part of motherhood,
that my desire to keep you safe never ends.

B. G. Thurston

INVOLUNTARY CRAFTSMANSHIP

I fear, my tiny replica of God,
your miniature precision
spurs in me an egotism—
that my body formed a thing as you,
admittedly of plans and mold divine,
yet executed still by this same flesh
and sinew that encompass lofty thought.
To think, as I was churning milk to waste,
coughing in the night and sleeping late,
I was engaged in art to make
the masters shrink in disbelief;
involuntary craftsmanship
no Persian rug could match in symmetry
with unschooled spontaneity
no primitive wood carving could approach,
no ancient Chinese urn compare
in delicate pure form.
Imagine how, as I was waddling
awkwardly and large,
my blood and breath and vitamins
and genes of generations
were silently, expertly sculpting you—
a task with all the grace

of living swans
and dying saints,
an artistry to humble blest Renoir,
in scope to rival pyramids,
in impact to match the holy books
of all the world.
How can I now be satisfied
with needlework or poetry,
my perfect child of God,
my love, and me,
since we created you?

Maureen Tolman Flannery

NEWBORN

Her head is nestled deep into my shoulder,
her body having melted into the mold of my chest.
One chubby fist still opens and closes,
clutching folds of my gown and releasing them again.
She smells of mountain air after a rain.
I rest my lips on her silky hair
and move them back and forth—
more a gesture of sensual delight
for my lips, than a kiss whispered
on the perfect, tactile fur of her drowsy head.

Maureen Tolman Flannery

3

Babyhood

MOTHER TONGUE

In the trailer park
where diapers snap on clotheslines
like flags in semaphore
the child cradled in my arms
lies swaddled in
the rhythms of her world.

She hears a thrush song
from the thicket
and searches with her eyes.
Bird I tell her
and wish her wings.

And when she shivers to the breeze
that shakes pine needles
from their boughs
I whisper *wind*
and wish her grace.

She looks to me
while sprinkles dance staccato
on our metal roof.
Rain I say
and wish her gentleness.

She gathers all these sounds of life
like nosegays edged in baby's breath
and stores them in her throat.
Then, in a voice
as soft as summer showers
meadow music
whiffs of wind

she names me *Mama*.

Regina Murray Brault

BRIT HA-HAYIM

Daughter, I name you with my breath.
I name you with the rhythm of my heart.
Each letter of your name pulses,
the first letter alive
with my own mother's name.
I name you daughter of daughter
of my mother. I name you
daughter of daughter of daughter
of daughter of your grandmother's
grandmother, the first letter
of her name still buzzing
alive inside of you.
I name you daughter of breath.
I name you daughter of heart.
I name you daughter of this family.
I name you daughter.

Gayle Brandeis

THE NAMING

We named you
for the sake of tradition.
The rabbi said a blessing,
grandparents cried
as great-grandparents live on
in your name.

We named you
for your great-grandmother
who was the first to assimilate
when she changed her name,
on Ellis Island.

We named you
for the dark eyes
I dreamed you'd have
just like your father.

We named you
for what you'd become
whatever the outcome.
We placed our hope
in your hopes, before
you were born.

We named you
for the song
that will remember
everything: Yiddish
Hebrew, broken English,
all rolled into one voice
that belongs to a world of faith.

Susan Fridkin

NURSING

Each night now with my gown undone,
flannel damp on my skin, my breasts
are revealed like waning moons.

Milk drops on her eyelashes
as her seeking mouth
signals its need.
We fumble,
steer through the darkness
toward one another—
we meet in the fullness.

Andrea Potos

WAITING TO HEAL

How heavy your breath comes
in the dark with only
my powerless hands
to hold you.
How slow your recovery
arrives.
No darker night,
no deeper love
than waiting for you
to heal.

Corrine De Winter

BIRTH RIGHTS

You stir in the night.
I come to you—
embracing your tiny form,
gently pressing my face against yours;
breathing in that sweet indelible aroma of new life.
Your wordless pleas summon my soul.
You compel my breasts to sustain you.
Satiated, you lay fast asleep.
Gently rounded lips—
whitewashed with milk.
I rock you in silent maternal rapture.
A wonder too rich to fathom,
cradled helplessly in my arms;
a bond beyond mere genetics.
Sacred union.
You are my flesh,
I am your keeper.

Jill Noblit MacGregor

BABY STEPS

In your first pair of shoes
You go off on your own
And I haven't a clue
Where the journey will end.
Though you reach for my hand
As you stumble and fall
Less and less you return
For a kiss and a hug.
No surprise I admit
To the plan underfoot
Still you're moving so fast
Like the hands of the clock
Till I want to cry "Stop!"
But I know that's not right
So I'm cheering you on
While you're walking away.

Rosalie Calabrese

GROWING DAUGHTER

Oh, how I grip
   the back of the sofa
As I watch you bob
   and weave
      and eventually tumble

Cautious first steps
   must be your own
The hardest part
   of that lesson
      is mine alone

Mary Maude Daniels

4

Toddlerhood

BEYOND WORDS

No words
will ever describe
my heart, overflowing
when your three-year-old legs
carry you, running
into my arms, and your soft,
chubby arms
squeeze around my neck, tightly
as you whisper in my ear
"My Mommy."

Cheryl Morikawa

SMALL OFFERINGS

In my overgrown garden, I weed,
trying to untangle a season of neglect.
Across the yard, from an old hose,
my daughter collects water into
cupped hands and slowly
walks the offering toward me.
The liquid dribbles between soft
fingers, sprinkles small bare feet.

She arrives, arms stretched high
then sees she has nothing to give me.
My gloved finger points to her toes
glistening with the lost drops
and tears begin to form.
Leaning down, I bring her hands
to my lips and swallow all
her empty drink and whisper,
    pretend water is so much sweeter.

                                        Kim Konopka

THE CAT'S MEOW

I guess I was hoping my daughter's first sentence
Would include me, that when she graduated
From grunts and puffs, she would produce
A sentence that mentioned Mommy.

But her first sentence was a question,
An inquiry of utmost import to her:
"Where kitty go?" she asked.

Martha K. Baker

Taking a Nap

It is evening and she
lies half-naked beside me
in the antique bed.
Suddenly, she is more
beautiful than the moon.
Her eyes, bouldered deep
into her father's blue,
are shut
like two perfect wings.

My shadow spreads
like a fan over her sleeping
face. I touch
her hair. I
kiss her head.

Where does the earth find
such girls? How does the sun
come down to braid
such yellow into
this girl's hair?
All the birds in the world
have visited her tongue.
She is a basket full of lemons
near a river in September.
She is a forest.

She runs through
the house spilling sand
from her pockets, spilling
feathers and music and
angels from her shoes.
She comes to my summer
skirt in the kitchen singing:
Mama, you smell like celery!

She walks
on Technicolor legs
among all the sounds of the living.
Look at the purple stories on her hands.

Sarah Fox

FAMILY SAMPLER

"You'll poke your eyes out"
was the litany of my childhood—
the warnings against sticks, stones,
and broken bones; the woods—
who knew what lurked
in the hearts of trees
with their wild black arms
and broken dreams?
Caution was stitched into samplers;
safety embroidered in counted cross-stitch.
I learned to never talk with wolves,
peek into cottages, taste greener grass.
Today, the sun diamonds the snow;
the surface crust is hardpack, glare ice.
You're only two, my youngest daughter,
but fear's not on your word list.

We climb our neighbor's sloping yard,
I push off, my small blue spinner,
and watch you whirl wildly
on your round red disk,
freed from gravity,
giddy and unafraid.
And yet heartstill
I hear the litany—
"the edge, the tree,
those coming rocks."

Barbara Crooker

There Are Times in Life When
One Does the Right Thing

the thing one will not regret,
when the child wakes crying "Mama," late
as you are about to close your book and sleep
and she will not be comforted back to her crib,
she points you out of her room, into yours,
you tell her, "I was just reading here in bed,"
she says, "Read a book," you explain it's not a children's book
but you sit with her anyway, she lays her head on your breast,
one-handed, you hold your small book, silently read,
resting it on the bed to turn pages
and she, thumb in mouth, closes her eyes, drifts,
not asleep—when you look down at her, her lids open,
and once you try to carry her back
but she cries, so you return to your bed again and book,
and the way a warmer air will replace a cooler with a slight
shift of wind, or swimming, entering a mild current, you
enter this pleasure, the quiet book, your daughter in your lap,
an articulate person now, able to converse, yet still
her cry is for you, her comfort in you,
it is your breast she lays her head upon,
you are lovers, asking nothing but this bodily presence.
She hovers between sleep, you read your book,

you give yourself this hour, sweet and quiet beyond flowers
beyond lilies of the valley and lilacs even, the smell of her
   breath,
the warm damp between her head and your breast. Past
   midnight
she blinks her eyes, wiggles toward a familiar position,
utters one word, "sleeping." You carry her swiftly into her crib,
cover her, close the door halfway, and it is this sense of
   rightness,
that something has been healed, something
you will never know, will never have to know.

Ellen Bass

EVERYTHING LEAVES TRACES

Cross-legged she sits
watching me wash my hair.
She doesn't speak when
fragrant foam covers
my head, or as I rinse
and towel dry. Reaching
her tiny arms upward,
I lift her, and as we
leave the room she
whispers into my moist
hair: "Mommy, you smell good."

Lois Greene Stone

GIFTS

Of all the small things we are given to love—
new grass, acorns, the mystery of seeds,
February's warm breath, raspberries, lilacs in the spring—
I love you most of all
because you have given them back to me.
A keen eye for the moon,
gentle fingers tracing a sidewalk's crack,
the lacy web of a fly's wing.
You have taught me to taste the world again,
swallow dry snow,
smell the surprise of the January sun.
You, my small scientist of beauty,
recover the wonder of life
in your open, astonished hands.

Sheila O'Connor

5

Childhood

WAIT

How
did you outgrow this picture so fast—
bald and beaming
your tiny, diapered tush
wiggling and waddling
down the hall,
back so small;

now so big
blonde and beautiful
fancy that you're five;

you ask,
"How soon
before I'm a teenager?"

I BEG,
"wait, little girl,
please wait."

Pamela L. Laskin

Morning Vows

Last night you flung your sleepy body in my bed
I raised your weight, half breath against my cheek
to return you to your bed
rough sea of dreams
where one arm noosed around my neck
you pinned me down,
murmured from deep sleep
"I love you, Mom."

"Me too," I whispered back.
"You're safe and sound."

Then, palming gentle
circles on your chest
I watched until the flutter of your lids,
and heavy breath
returned to you some calm.

But, now this morning we've left our dark behind
not even memory.
You only want to read how seal pups
stay with their mother until they can catch fish.
Departure so dependent on survival.

I ask you how long you'll need to stay with me.
"Until eighteen."
I'm amazed. "That's right." I say.
"And then you'll go away."
"But I'll come home. You can write that down."
"Write what?" I ask.
"The dates, I'm coming back. Don't forget."

I turn away to blink. Peculiar species of love
suppose we'll all survive.
You grind your elbow sharp into my rib
press your sweet flesh of summer sweat
ripe peach against my skin and ask,

"You will remember me?"

Oh yes.

Sheila O'Connor

LEARNING TO READ

Sprawled across the couch like an afghan,
still in flannel nightie, auburn hair
disheveled from tussling with dream demons,
she calls me over. I expect perhaps to be shown
an almost invisible fairy hovering
above a leaf in her picture book.
Listen, she says, with the authority
of one who knows she knows something.
There was on, onk…once a k, king…
She's memorized this, I tell myself.
with a love, lovely and dis, disob-ede…disobedient…
She gets a foothold on *disobedient*
and climbs over it like a sturdy stone fence
never meant to keep out neighbors.
dag, dag-ter, daughter, w…wom, whom he wished
Future muscles in, elbowing out her babyhood.
to mar, marry a prink, prince of his own choos-ing.
This changes everything. Her early childhood
gone on the air with the breathy giggles
that chased the rabbits around the yard. Now Plato,
Dante, Shakespeare can whisper to her soul…
and so can so many others with so much less to say.
Nutritional info on cereal boxes will complicate

her breakfast. Moving marquees outside banks
will conduct their unilateral dialogues with her
daydreams. *National Enquirers* in the grocery store
will spit their sibilant lies into her nights.
Traffic signs won't seem like ruby crystal slices
or designs the color of black-eyed Susans.
The Shell logo won't remind her of the seaside.
Now everywhere she looks someone I do not know
will be telling her what she should want.
I hold her on the couch and we laugh and cry
for we can't bring back the knight's shield
that from now on will only denote highways.

Maureen Tolman Flannery

SEPARATION

Another stormy morning
full of snarls and screams
about clothes that don't fit,
moaning about a stomach ache,
meaning that I don't care, that no one
cares you are nine, and finding your way.

Your hair's a knotted net;
you'd think I draw blood as I brush.
It would look so nice short, and yet
that's *my* mother talking, not us—
you and I who were so close, who breathed
the same air, and now simmer and seethe.

O anger's everywhere, the way
you set your jaw like a stubborn carp
or a northern pike, whose place
is in the reedy deep. The stars
that prick this night won't light
our path. I can't hold you—
you've grown bony and slight,
slipping from me. Soon
you will be gone from here,
my lilac girl, born in May.
The wind blows freer
than we do, and pale
purple stars cover the earth.

Barbara Crooker

THE FIVE-YEAR CHANGE

She turns from me
and slouches against the wall.
"I'm sooo tired of my mom..."
This summer she is
higher than my navel.
She can tie her shoelaces
and spell her last name.
She is growing out her bangs,
and they drape her pinched face
in black.

She kicks the baby's toy
across the floor and restates
her contempt, third person
and a little louder. "Boy,
do I *hate* my mom."
Her words shatter
on the unswept kitchen floor
as if they were made of glass.
All this because of French toast
which I will not make
when the rest of us
are eating oatmeal.

As she speaks, I can almost see
the angry cigarette dangling
from the corner of her full lips,
only recently, it seems,
weaned from my body.
A trail of smoke floats
out her nostrils and up
into my face: tears
she refuses to cry.

Peggy Hong

I HATE BROCCOLI

I yelled, "I hate broccoli" but
my mother forced me to eat it
anyway.
My nose started to twitch,
itch,
wiggle and run. So did I—
right up to my room
for a tissue. As soon as I
got to my room, I sneezed a
loud,
humongous sneeze that pushed
my bed
across the room, made my chair
float
up to the ceiling, blew down
my shades,
shoved my sofa out the window,
and updrafted my desk. What a
mess!
Guess what my mother said??
"What a big achoo. Clean your room!
And God bless you."

Jennifer Shunfenthal, age 10

TO MY DAUGHTER,
WEARING HER FATHER'S SHOES

Almost six, you shuffle
into view—dragging a briefcase
delicate bare legs disappearing
into heroic oxfords.

Daughter, don't hurry so
to trade barefoot freedom—
tiptoeing, eyes squinched shut
thinking you're invisible—for
taxes, creditors, and mortgages.

Daughter, listen to me:
wiggle free from those shoes now
hop like a froggy for the pond
prance like a circus pony and
leap for the fireflies of dusk.

SuzAnne C. Cole

A Child's Surgery

Her spirit cloisters
against white dragons that
snarl pain into dreams.

I hold her childhood
and murmur small words
into the grey of her eyes,

hear the questions
piled in her palms
as they stretch

against new assaults
of white-coat warriors
with trolleyed swords.

I cannot touch
her lonely hurt
into my experience;

I cannot breathe for her
and take these fears
into my own nightmares.

Joanna M. Weston

A PROMISE TO MY SICK CHILD

When I was sick
my mother would sit by my bed,
all night if she had to,
rubbing my temple with a cool washcloth.
My daughter,
I promise to do the same for you.
You will hear my voice
soothe you back to sleep,
in the darkness feel me massage
your precious hands and feet,
cover your body with all my love
until you are well again.

Mary Eastham

DAUGHTER

I cannot fathom
the depth of you.
Your brother's thoughts
are visible in their actions.
When the boys are quiet
they are probably conniving.
When you are silent
you are deepening,
ripening.

The boys ask hundreds of questions.
You come to me with answers and
explanations you have shaped.
You bring games you have devised
drawings you designed
with the instructions on how it came to be
color, shapes, construction.

I already see the woman deep inside of you
as complex as your life will be.
So much will be expected of you who are
bright, beautiful and wise.
My own wisdom already seems limited
compared to yours.
What have I to offer
You who have so many answers.
I am sure you will teach me.
I have so much to learn.

Sherri Waas Shunfenthal

THE CONVERSATION

My stepdaughter-to-be has found a snail
and lets it travel her arm.
"Look," she says. "Isn't it sweet?"

She explains that if it were scared,
the antennae would not be extended.

She waits patiently
while the snail traverses her arm,

which is brown with summer,
smooth as a snail's shell.

We have so far to go.
We have come this far.

Kelly Cherry

SIDE BY SIDE

Side by side
With my daughter
Making a cake from scratch

Flour
Butter
Water
Eggs

Sugar to add sweetness
To our day
We stir and stir

Memories
Myself as a little girl
Baking joyfully with my mother
Side by side

Sherri Waas Shunfenthal

My Mother Is the Best

My mother's hands are soft
as a cat's fur.
When I hug my mother
she feels like a bird's feathers.
Her kisses and hugs are so big.
They are as big as elephants.
Best of all I love her.

Jennifer Shunfenthal, age 7

GRAVITY

Carrying my daughter to bed
I remember how light she once was,
no more than a husk in my arms.
There was a time I could not put her down,
so frantic was her crying if I tried
to pry her from me, so I held her
for hours at night, walking up and down the hall,
willing her to fall asleep. She'd grow quiet,
pressed against me, her small being alert
to each sound, the tension in my arms, she'd take
my nipple and gaze up at me,
blinking back fatigue she'd fight whatever terror
waited beyond my body in her dark crib. Now
that she's so heavy I stagger beneath her,
she slips easily from me, down
into her own dreaming. I stand over her bed,
fixed there like a second, dimmer star,
though the stars are not fixed: someone
once carried the weight of my life.

Kim Addonizio

My Daughter, Ten, Dresses As an Alien

This Halloween she doesn't want to see herself
in Princess pink and gold, in Emerald Lady gleam
of Oz, even last year's sparkled onyx satin
Woman Who Came From the Night Storm Sky.
No—"nothing pretty this time," she says, and so
we search for weeks for just the right mask,
a dream of bulging opalescence, huge eyes
that make the planets small, the world a frail
glass marble. Black pants, black silvered jacket,
sleek black shoes set to step through space,
and from her neck a braided ribbon of light
holding a single perfect circle she'll use
to draw others to her power. Dusk comes,
the pumpkins we've cut into demons and cats
glow against time's grin. Before candy,
before the doors that will open and close,
I photograph her where she once stood pretty,
this daughter, my creature, her strange new face
turned upward towards the reachable moon.

Katharyn Howd Machan

I SHOULD BE SO LUCKY

I see my daughter looking
at us, side by side, as if we're two pieces
of her jigsaw puzzle.
She looks for sameness; she searches for
identifiable differences.

Finally
She tells me:
>   *Mom! You have your mama's voice.*
>   *Mom! You have your mama's hands.*
>   *Mom! You have your mama's smile.*
She laughs:
>   *Mom! You're turning into your mama!*
I laugh back:
>   *I should be so lucky.*

Jane Butkin Roth

The Way She Greets the Day

The way she bounces down the stairs—
the way I'm struck by the joyous sound of her—
as she yells, *What's for breakfast?*
It's the way she greets the day—
and listens for my shout back: *Waffles!*
and the way she yells, *Yippee!*—
sends a prayer
  to my heart

for on an ordinary day
in our ordinary house
my extraordinary girl breathes life into our
  small unnoticed routines.

It's the way we change, more alive
through the simple pure heart of a child—
the way she quickly takes inventory
and concludes all is good;
it's the way she greets the day.

Jane Butkin Roth

6

Adolescence

My Middle Daughter, on the Edge of Adolescence, Learns to Play the Saxophone

Her hair, that halo of red gold curls,
has thickened, coarsened,
lost its baby fineness,
and the sweet smell of childhood
that clung to her clothes
has just about vanished.
Now she's getting moody,
moaning about her hair,
clothes that aren't the right brands,
boys that tease.
She clicks over the saxophone keys
with gritty fingernails polished in pink pearl,
grass stains on the knees
of her sister's old designer jeans.
She's gone from sounding like the smoke detector
through "Old MacDonald" and "Jingle Bells."
Soon she'll master these keys,
turn notes into liquid gold,
wail that reedy brass.
Soon, she'll be a woman.
She's gonna learn to play the blues.

Barbara Crooker

Rites of Passage

My daughter takes her driving test,
and I wait by the fence,
chained by all the old fears.
She drives off with the inspector,
squinty eyed, critical.
Be kind, I pray, this is my little girl.
I glimpse them in the distance,
traversing the maze of stop signs, yields,
pylons. She pivots into the k-turns,
grips the wheel too tight.
From this distance, they could be on a ride
in an amusement park: The Flying Dutchman,
The Wild Mouse, The Runaway Train.
She's white-lipped with fear & pleasure;
I'm down here on earth, stomach in a fist,
fear tap dancing staccato on my heart.
They never told me in the hospital
that this cord could not be cut.
The silver car returns, bringing them back.

He tips his hat, hands her the forms.
She passes! She's a driver!
And off we go, careening through
the rest of our tangled lives.

Barbara Crooker

SUITABLE OCCUPATIONS FOR
MOTHERS OF ADOLESCENTS

I am now the age
my mother was
when she began to be stupid
and embarrass me,
when I began to realize
the only socially acceptable
origin was to have hatched
independently from an egg,
to have no mother at all,
or, if you must, only one
who abandoned you
in early childhood
to conduct photographic
safaris, dive for sunken galleons,
or scale Everest.

Maureen Tolman Flannery

CONSECRATION

I was thirteen when I gave my mother
a small wicker basket of talcum powders,
bath gel and rosewater. Handling each bottle
like a semi-precious stone, she placed them on
the bathroom counter like an altar-offering.

Ashamed of my own body, I was the moon, wanting
to show myself only when the world was black.
I watched her undress and saw her familiar body.
A thick pink scar stretched across
the place where her left breast should have been.

She filled the sink with warm soapy waters,
drowning a sponge until it was heavy with water,
then rubbed her skin clean, sprinkled and smoothed
my gifts onto her body, anointing and preparing herself.

I do not remember if we ever spoke.
I knew only the touch of light on our bodies.

Andrea O'Brien

THROUGH THE EYES OF HER CHILD

Her outstretched hand,
was silken and smooth,
yet rough and tired,
from holding up our house.
She called to me,
with a familiar voice;
such a calm and soothing tone.
Her scent was
as native as flowers.
It was sweet-smelling and fragrant,
yet not stored in any bottle or spray.
She would lock me up in her arms.
Her violet sweater,
was old, worn and faded,
but still soft against my cheek.
No matter how hot or cold,
it was outside,
she was always
the right temperature.

Kathryn Byron, age 16

PROM NIGHT

Behold the fair lady.
Out in the hall.
When did she blossom?
I can't recall.
Why is she gowned
In white eyelet and lace…
Her hair done in curls,
A glow on her face?
Who is the young man
Coming to call…
To take my Cinderella
Away to the ball?
Who are these children
Of years so tender?
One of them's mine,
Whom I must surrender.

Madonna Dries Christensen

SOMETIMES

Sometimes I look at her, and she will
remind me of someone familiar.
Sometimes I'm upset with her,
because she is not enough like me,
then other times I fear she is.
Sometimes I watch her hands,
do things women do and I think,
everything is moving too fast.
Sometimes I have a fierce urge
to hold her in my arms,
and try to hold back the future.
Sometimes when I look at her, she takes
my breath away because she is so pretty.
Sometimes I want to cry for this
girl-woman child of mine,
for what might be ahead of her.

Sometimes I'm afraid,
because as she grows I seem
to get smaller, as if her beginning
means my end.
Sometimes I ache for the child she
once was, and other times,
I can't wait for the woman
she will be...
My Daughter

Christina Keenan

INITIATION

Last night, dear daughter,
You cried your first grown-up tears.
Tears that sprang from a broken heart,
You said you could tell the moment it cracked.

These tears weren't
Begot by frustration,
Or anger,
Or lack of sleep.
They were tears of initiation.
Tears that told you
The world can be a cruel place,
Life isn't always fair,
and that the cost for living is suffering alone.

Last night, dear daughter,
You cried your first grown-up tears.
And, in the darkness,
If you had listened,
You would have heard
The echo of my heart cracking, too.

Joan Shea O'Neal

BIRTH PANGS REDUX

One day the house sings of lullabies
and tea parties, dolly chatter,
the next, cranked-up discord
and doors that slam ten times a day,
and I realize with sinking heart
I've spawned a teen, a child
more fragile than an unborn babe,
for now mother shelter is outgrown.
Like a butterfly, this new creature,
this lady-child, has to beat against her cocoon
to make wings strong enough to fly.
I squint, tear-eyed, into the horizon,
knowing one day she will soar
to unimaginable heights, a
promise that lifts my eyes from
clothes on the floor, pierced body parts
and what passes as music, and
sets me free to pause in her doorway
and applaud each flailing effort
to grow up and away.

Margaret Anne Huffman

UNCHANGED

Sliding into cold slippers,
I shuffled, opened the
refrigerator door, removed
a cold bottle and yawned.
Babies grow, I reasoned,
and noted two A.M.

Sliding into cold slippers,
I shuffled, listened for
the door latch, yawned,
and noted two A.M.
My baby grew into a
teenager.

Lois Greene Stone

7

Leaving Home

THE COURAGE TO BE

She hovers at the brink of change,
Heart pounding wildly
Like a caged bird
Longing to sing.

Oh for the notes to flow
Smoothly, easily.
Oh for a song already composed!

Quivering, wanting
To beat her wings hard,
To fly free,
She sits on her silent perch

While courage mounts
For that first flight
Into the unknown.

Susan Landon

ME 'N' BRUCE SPRINGSTEEN TAKE
MY BABY OFF TO COLLEGE

(The length of time to drive from Allentown to Pittsburgh is the same
length of time it takes to play the entire *Bruce Springsteen Live* tapes, with
a little *Tunnel of Love* mixed in.)

We hit the turnpike early, O Thunder Road,
every inch of the car packed: sweatshirts, prom gowns,
books, teddy bears, such heavy baggage.
She's both coming and going, this shy violet of a child,
the teenager too hostile to be in the same room, breathe the
    same air.
Now she dozes beside me as the car spools us the miles,
and I slip in a favorite tape, turn up the volume.
Her skin, edible, a downy peach, her long hair unwinding.
My foot taps the accelerator with the beat; the Big Man,
Clarence Clemons, pours his soul out his sax, yearning,
throbbing, as the turnpike pulls us west, bisecting
Pennsylvania, tunneling through the mountains: Blue,
Allegheny, Kittatinny, Tuscarora, this big-muscled,
broad-backed hunk of state.
We drive deeper into the heart of anthracite,
the wind blows through the dark night of her hair.
A harmonica wails and whines, brings me back to my tie-dyed

college years; sex looms like a Ferris wheel,
carnival lights in the water, but we've reached our exit,
here she is, it's independence day, ready or not,
Pittsburgh, city of smoke and grit, polished chrome
and glass, soot-streaked buildings, pocket-handkerchief
neighborhoods, abandoned steelworks, the Monongahela River.
I deliver her again, heavier this time.
We set up the room, she turns cocky and sulky,
breaks into sobs when I leave.
On the return trip, I play the same tapes over and over.
Vultures float in the mountain thermals, a black convoy, lacy
    flakes of char.
The miles roll by, I'm driven by the beat, everybody's got a
    hungry heart,
nearly there: Lenhartsville, Krumsville, Kutztown,
green rolling hills dotted with cows,
Pittsburgh's iron and steel filling the horizon in the rearview
    mirror.

Barbara Crooker

SAYING GOOD-BYE

When your flight was called for boarding yesterday, I was still not ready. We had arrived at the airport with time to spare. We checked in, bought you a donut and juice, and two additional rolls of film. Then we passed through the security area and proceeded to Gate A-2. For the next 45 minutes we sat side by side, each holding our huge emotions tethered to our hearts—yet speaking none of them aloud. It was only later, alone on my drive back home, that I reviewed all the words left unspoken between us. Did you know that this good-bye is but a dress rehearsal? Just before boarding the jet, you pressed your fingers against mine, looked me straight in the eye and said: *I'll be back, Mom. Don't worry, I'm coming back.* Those fingers of yours, still so slender and smooth—mine so stubby and creviced. And suddenly everything was reversed between us, you comforting me as if I were the child and you the adult. Your words, your fingers, your eyes, all poised to protect me—to stave off the hole tearing into my heart—your leaving, now, a few months from now again, a year and a half from now once more—this fierce love of mine for you, my first-born daughter, what will I do with it once you've gone?

Stephanie B. Palladino

STRENGTH

We're saying goodbye again
In a new dorm room
As I prepare to start my third year of college.
It never gets any easier does it?
I remember saying goodbye my freshman year.
You held my father's hand when he wept
And I remember thinking,
Who will hold your hand when you miss me?
Who will be your strength while I'm here?

I'm different from when I started this adventure, Mom,
But I have learned a few things.
As I sit and compose endless e-mails to you,
Sending my frustrations and my triumphs
Over this electronic umbilical cord,
I realize that even though you don't hear my voice every day,
My hastily typed snippets sustain us
And keep us close.
I am your daughter.

I am your strength
As you are mine.

Danielle Brigante

PARENTS' DAY ON CAMPUS

Smoothly over the swells,
she sails in our direction.

She tacks toward us, a clipper,
trim yet akimbo with her signals.

That's your grin, waves of wild hair,
oceans within eyes filled with joy.

I brace myself against her energy.
Your hair is nice and shiny, I coo.

Seaweed shampoo, she replies coolly,
slurping a Snapple, circling our harbor.

Her jeans dance like new flags
of her own countries, sunny, strong.

Mary Kennan Herbert

VISITOR

The daughter drops in from her college world,
not to reclaim her place
in the orbit of home
but to etch her presence,
spread energy and socks
like uncorked champagne.

It will be this way...

She roams like a he-dog, makes sure we know...
a shoe in one room,
purse in another,
sweaters spill into the hall—
uncontrollable.

Always.

One day she collects her art book, makeup, disappears.
But after she's leapt back to her life,
her voice bounces off walls,
shoes seem to creep out
from under the beds,
breath lingers in dust
wrapped around sun.

Diane Sher Lutovich

WHEN DID I WEEP?

Not when I hugged you
goodbye
at a college dormitory,
a frightened, wide-eyed innocent;

Not when I waved you
farewell
at a crowded airport,
Paris-bound, an ingénue;

Not when I watched you
saunter
down the aisle, a grinning,
strong, new graduate;

But when I blew you a kiss
one ordinary Sunday
as you drove away
from home.

For then did I know
that the cutting
of the cord
had come,

and that your
sweet life
is everywhere
you are...but here.

Yes, then, in that
metaphorical moment
of goodbye, farewell,
Godspeed,
Then did I know,
And I wept.

Elayne Clift

LITTLE GIRL GROWN

Monday I tied blue ribbons in her hair
before she went to school.
Tuesday I packed her teddy bear
and she was off to camp.
Friday I drove her to college
with her silver flute.
Sunday she moved to Manhattan
with her fiancé.

Will the neighbors on East 35th Street
please see that she doesn't dawdle
on her way to work?
She's the one with the flute
and the teddy bear
and blue ribbons
in her hair.

Arlene L. Mandell

In Retrospect

Roads taken away from you are many.
Do not fear, Mother; they all lead back.
Not because I must, because I *can*
return, a woman in my own right,
lighter of heart for having made the journeys,
full of love for the chance
to be.

Arlene Gay Levine

8

Adulthood

BECOMING MY MOTHER

And suddenly it's her voice I'm speaking
with, it's her look that's in my eye, and I
can feel it there, as if her face were my
face, and even the gestures I am making
are ones that were characteristic of her—
an absent twisting of a strand of hair,
a hand across her mouth, a decided air
of disapproval or despair, whichever
she felt, because she was never any good
at hiding what she felt—and there we're different,
since one thing I learned was to be diffident,
my role, forever, not mother- but child- hood.
    But now I find myself becoming her;
    childless though I am, my own mother.

Kelly Cherry

TIME WARP

My daughter gives me advice these days
Unsolicited opinions on every subject
My appearance, for example
And how to run a household
How to get a man's attention
And how to keep it
Seems to know a great deal about everything
At nearly twenty-four
She doesn't mince words, either
As plainspoken, in fact
As ever I was in my youth:

Your hair's too long!
Your skirt's too short!
You can't wear that hat!
And you look terrible in that flowered dress!

You don't need more books!
You should get a new stove!
You should drink milk!
And you should never have given the cats away!
When did she start being the mother, I wonder
And just when did I become a child again?

Marguerite McKirgan

As I Watch My Daughter Marry

I remember her at eleven:
she will not let me love her,
slams the door between us,
wants to be grown so fast but
complains as her nipples widen,
soft and tender and aching.
I wish I could explain to her how
fast everything goes by and that I need
to slow it all down, but she is always
pushing for something more that she
imagines is a prize for being older and
we can never come to agreement over terms.

In a calm moment on her grandmother's back porch,
we discover an infant robin who flew too early
on the lawn under the box elder, bottom-heavy
like a diapered baby, its stick wings
working furiously, barely lifting it back up
toward its rough nest again and again.
Both of us afraid to touch the bird for fear
its mother might abandon it from our scent,
we watch the baby's struggle, cheering it on,
and my daughter slides
closer to me on the step.

Nita Penfold

WEDDING FAREWELL

The music for the Mother of the Bride began;
you hugged me rather fiercely,
kissed my cheek and said, "Good-bye."
Thinking of my new home
in the same block as yours, and
happily bewildered, I replied
"I'm not going anywhere."
You turned, much too quickly,
to be led off down the aisle.

Today is our second anniversary
and only just now it strikes me
how very far I was going.

Gail McCoig Blanton

A Note to My Husband's Mother

I will never forget the day when your friend
Asked, "Is this your new daughter-in-law?"
And you answered, "No, this is my new daughter."

Barbara Younger

A Father's View of Mother and Daughter

They will not let me in
These Two
When they talk frankly of
Hair
Skin
Eyes
Lights and shadows of
Entrapping strategies.

They will not let me in
These Two
When they hear distant sounds of
Melody
Lyrics
Song
Words and music of
Their private fantasies.

They will not let me in
These Two
When they seek balances of
Friendship
Romance
Love
On scented fulcrums of
Corsages pinned against the heart.

They will not let me in
These Two
When they whisper words of
Warning
Danger
Fear
Probabilities of
Numbers not to be ignored.

They will not let me in
These Two
When they share dreams of
Hope
Ambition
Destiny
Gossamer illusions
Too real to be reality.

They will not let me in
These Two—
But, then, there is no need for
Them to do so.

Their hearts and mine already intertwine.

Daniel Roselle

I TAKE YOUR *YES!* AND ECHO IT BACK

(For my mother)

Yes! I have more space inside
than any younger me, more room
for the rhythm of the song I sing today,
a song of you, the woman, my mother.
For years I tried to pin you down
with definitions limited
by my own dusty collection of memories,
but you, the presence, the being you are
have made it clear you're so much more.

I say *Yes!* to your legacy—
your fine taste, artist's eye,
magnet spirit drawing others near you,
delight in precious hours alone,
Yes! to your jumping into the river
of life and letting it take you
to places you hadn't imagined.

I take your *Yes!* and echo it back
to you and in the echoing the *Yes!*
grows bigger than the legacy itself—
so big it includes what we didn't want
to inherit or to pass on, so big
it includes what we've yet to understand.

Kathy Conde

9

Grandmotherhood

NEW LIFE

My daughter's belly
moves beneath my hand
The child within her stirring
stirs in me a rush of awe
of mystery
so strong
so primal in its source
I touch infinity

Maude Meehan

SACRAMENT

(While rocking a newborn grandchild at 4:00 A.M.)

I swaddle
    and rock you
my cheek
    to your brow.
We breathe grace
    to one another.
You leave your hand print
    on my soul
and with the balm
    of your baby scent
I am annointed
    as your grandmother.

Donna Wahlert

GRANDBABY

Sometimes, dear child, I forget
the exact expression
in your inquisitive brown eyes.
Other times I can't recall
the contour of your cherub-cheeks.
What precisely do your hands
look like—and your feet?
But my arms, like the collective
memory of every woman
who has held a cherished child,
know the weight, the warmth,
the feel, the love of holding you.
Always, a woman's arms remember.

Elizabeth B. Estes

GRANDMOTHER'S GIFTS

You were the only one
who could interpret baby talk,
you shared a special understanding.
She was always the first
grandchild to run into your arms,
stealing a kiss from your lips,
before you had the chance
to give it.

At three, she'd speed-dial
your house, day and night.
She never outgrew calling you;
grandmothers are good for gab,
and know how to make
wishes come true.
They also are great
at sleepovers too!

Upon your king-size bed
she looked so small, pulling
from the velvet bag, your costume jewelry.
Lying next to you
she let you adorn her ears with pearls
and slip rings on each finger.
You gave her roots, and wings.

Today, before we flew
home from Florida, she picked
an array of impatiens
and placed them in a plastic bag.
Bewildered, I asked, "Why?"
Her eyes would not meet mine
as she replied, "Tomorrow is Grandma's birthday.
I'm taking these home for her grave."

Susan Fridkin

GRANDMOTHER'S POWER

I'm not talking about the power to build bridges
the kind of power my granddaddy had

I am talking about the power to bake cakes
my grandmother's kind of power, the power of the pantry
what kind of food and how much gets stored

the power of the kitchen
who's got the say in what gets cooked and how

the power of the dining room
what goes on the table and how long it stays there

the power of the refrigerator
what gets left over and what goes to the dog

I'm talking about the kind of power
says chicken tonight, fried and dripping with melted fat

power that says green beans, fresh from the garden
boiled up with bacon and onions

power that says canned biscuits tonight
instead of homemade
says iced tea with three tablespoons of sugar

power that says pound cake
smothered in berries, I picked them myself

my grandmother's kind of power said
you come to me when you're feeling hungry
you come to me when you're feeling weak
you come to me, and I'm going to feed you
I *am* the food that you eat

Alice Evans

10

Later Years

AFRICAN VIOLETS

(For my mother at 95)

She used to know the loving language
of violets. She spoke in low tones,
tipped water into them
from a copper can with a long spout.
Later, she'd empty
the saucer beneath each plant.
There were twenty on her tea cart
in the sunny window.
Fifteen were blooming any day you came.

Her fingers hover. She lifts a plant up,
turns it slowly in her hand, pulls off a dark leaf.
She no longer knows what to say
to the stubborn violet, the one that's held on.

Linda Goodman Robiner

LOVING HANDS

These rough and gnarled hands
once labored
long and lovingly
with knitting needles
to stitch soft sweaters
for small children to nestle into

These idle hands
once busy as
flitting butterflies
flew with needle and thread
to design drapes for our home
pillows for our chairs

These clumsy hands
once spirited and strong
kneaded and baked breads
cakes and pies to fill our home
with luscious smells

These awkward hands
once graceful
planted, weeded
grew tulips, roses
tomatoes, zucchini
in our backyard

These tired hands
that once grasped the fullness of life
hold lovely memories when
enfolded by the warmth
of my daughter's loving hands

Sherri Waas Shunfenthal

NOTE OF ADVICE TO THE GOOD NURSE, DEATH

My mother will never die in the fall
because king apples need polishing then,
need peeling round and round
in one continuous skin for eating by the fire.

She would refuse to die in winter
because pussy willows bud in December,
and purple violets make promises
beneath brown leaves.

Nor would Mother let go of this earth
in spring when tulips and daffodils,
first swallows and asparagus
come to her garden.

Your only chance, Good Nurse, will be
to come for Mother in summer,
a cool drink in your hand
a soothing salve in your apron pocket.

I've seen her fan herself
with her straw hat in August
beside the well when the water is low
and the deer flies are biting.

Thelma J. Palmer

CARTOGRAPHER

I stroke her papery skin
now lined, worn tissue thin
as ancient maps
Trace with my aging hands
seamed furrows of my mother land
Explore the future

Maude Meehan

11

Illness

New Game Song

Propped in a chair
there sits a pale lady
quavery white-haired
wisp of a lady
who made up the games
I played as a child

She has disguised
the strong hands
that held me
gnarled them like gingerroot
knotted with pain

See how she plays now
pretends not to know me
pretends she's forgotten
even my name

Mother
please tell me
the rules to this game

Maude Meehan

WAITING

The nurse
marks an appointment.
It is my daughter's name
she writes. Once more
the bow is drawn
the arrow aimed
at one of mine.
I wait for word.
The surgeon's verdict
finds its target
in my child;
it pierces me.
I cannot come to terms,
make peace with possibilities
that fracture reason.
I leave the house, go out
into the windswept day, bitter
to see the rainlashed trees
lose early blossoms.

Pacing the cliffs
I sense erosion
as wave on wave
sucks at the shore.

Along the far horizon, storm clouds
squat gray and swollen, waiting.

Maude Meehan

BEFORE MY GRANDDAUGHTER'S SURGERY

A thousand miles away from you
I do not know where to turn.
I visit the Trappistine Monastery,
then sit on a bench by their small lake.
I read, I pray, I contemplate.

An anhinga hangs from a fallen tree
drying out like a sail in the wind.
A snakebird darts under
the water like a crafty fish;
A salamander separates from his tail,
then scampers away.

Thoughts of you beat in me
like the snowy egret's wings.
I think of your tiny body,
that mite of kidney,
that thread of tubing tangled
like knitting yarn.

These minutes, these hours hang
like that still anhinga. I want to dive
with you into the smooth cool lake.
I want us to separate from the pain
like the salamander. I want to run
with you to a safer place.

Donna Wahlert

Recipe for Grief

My grandmother is dying in the hospital.
I cannot comprehend these words,
cannot feel grief, not yet.
Instead, I cut eggplant in a sunny kitchen,
dust it, pat each slice gently.
The flour is as fine and white as her skin.
I enter the ritual:
from flour to eggs to crumbs to oil,
moving in a pattern old as Napoli.
Working against burns and spills,
I assemble the golden slices,
alike as a party of aunts,
tomato sauce fragrant
with basil, oregano,
creamy mozzarella,
pungent parmesan.
In the heat of the oven,
they will meld
into something unlike the sum of their parts.

I've heard her voice in every direction,
her hands are working in mine,
as we create sundrenched Italy, ancient hills of thyme.
Fragrance steams from the oven, as the heady flavors mingle:
this parmigiana, this sacrament, this easing of the heart.

Barbara Crooker

THE MOST BEAUTIFUL LILY IN HEAVEN

MaMa.

She is cinnamon toast, lemon icebox pie, and chocolate pudding
made in a skillet.

She is baby's breath, violets, and morning glories.

She is the sound of the wind blowing through the sycamore
trees and the fresh smell of pine needles.

She is mud pies and walnuts—allowing me far too much
freedom, but knowing I loved her desperately because she
did.

She is the person who always answered when I called her name
from the back screen door.

She is the caretaker who calmly read while a preoccupied little
girl asked why there is a tiny mole in the middle of her neck.

She is a reminder of all that is good in the world—a soul that
has seen much pain and sadness yet remained forever kind.

She is the very best gift I was ever given as a child—flesh of her
flesh—I only pray I have a fraction of her heart.

Time robbed me of my precious gift not by taking her body but
by stealing her mind.

Her memory of me may have vanished, but I know a part of me
still lives somewhere inside.

As I sit beside her bed—her every breath a struggle—I pray she
feels no pain.

I knew this was coming.

I thought I was ready.

But the moment I saw her, I became a little girl again not wanting to go home.

Please, please let me stay!

I will reluctantly go, but my world will be forever changed.

I hope she can sense how very much I love her—how blessed I have been to have had her in my world—how blessed we all have been to have lived in hers.

Mona Davis

LADIES AND GENTLEMEN

(From *Mourning Pictures*)

Ladies and gentlemen, my mother is
dying. You say, "Everyone's mother dies."
I bow to you, smile. Ladies, gentlemen,
my mother is dying. She has cancer.
You say, "Many people die of cancer."
I scratch my head. Gentle ladies, gentle
men, my mother has cancer, and, short of
some miracle, will die. You say, "This has
happened many times before." You say, "Death
is something which repeats itself." I bow.
Ladies and gentlemen, my mother has cancer
all through her. She will die unless there's a
miracle. You shrug. You gave up religion
years ago. Marxism too. You don't believe
in anything. I step forward. My mother
is dying. I don't believe in miracles.
Ladies and gentlemen, one last time: My
mother's dying. I haven't got another.

Honor Moore

HERITAGE

Mother
how frail you are,
bent like a question mark.
The answer in your eyes.
White hair, milkweed down,
I blow and wish on it,
my wish denied.

I watch as you slowly
drift from us,
slowly let go.
Pure essence remains,
your life force, love.
Old one, dear one,
you will not leave us empty.

Maude Meehan

12

Partings

A WISH OF MINE

(Written one month after my mother died)

Some people say they don't know what they have
until it goes away,
but I will never feel that way,
because I appreciated her every day.
As I look around me
everyone seems to have a perfect home,
as I just sit here and feel so deeply alone.
No one ever talks to me.
They smile and pretend everything's okay
while I'm screaming inwardly
because I have so much to say.
How I dream this all
would not have happened to me,
but my friends say everything
that goes on was supposed to be.
My real wish is that this will make me strong
and that the pain will go away.
Oh, how I appreciated her every single day!

Ellen Sherck, age 12

ONE OF THE HARDEST THINGS

I remember one of the hardest things
in my teenage years was listening to my friends
complain about their mothers,
and I would cry inside,
thinking,
If only I had a mother.

June Cotner Graves

VIATICUM FOR A YOUNG DAUGHTER

You must tell her in words
quick-time what
had you long time
you would tell her with your life:

That because of her, you have no regrets,
although your grief is great; that
but for her, you would not be
and what's still undone is hers to do.

Free her to forgive, to make her way,
for justice and mercy cannot be gauged
where loss is part of gain. Free her
to believe we can go beyond,

And tell her you'll wait
in that boundary-less place
where All is right here Now.

Maryanne Hannan

CONTINUUM

Almost a year has passed
since you let go of life.
Spring comes.
Outside the window
small migrant birds
move delicate as grace notes
on the wire. I watch a sparrow
pull dead twigs from the porch vine
to weave into its nest below the eaves.
A daughter's belly swells,
a grandchild moves toward life,
and you are present for me
in this promise, in these affirmations.

Maude Meehan

PINK PEARLS

You had withered,
leaving behind shallow breath,
a shell of bone and me.
Our long conversations were nearly over,
the only sounds between us the
hum of a morphine pump.

Rachel was just three,
too young to know the way of death.
I, soon to be motherless,
was her faltering guide.
So I let her climb into your hospital bed
and hold your hand.

"Grandma needs her nails done,
she likes them pretty!" Rachel reminded me.
I found a bottle of Pink Pearl by the rosary beads
in your nightstand.
I took the beads, Rachel the polish
and we set to our work.

I prayed, she manicured
and when we were through,
Rachel slipped into your still arms
for one last nap. I, less
certain of what to do,
could only look away.

It's been ten years since that bleak December's day.
Rachel is thirteen now,
a graceful, wildflower girl.
When I touch her hands, hands long and tapered,
nails bright like yours, I touch you.
And know that life, once withered, is now in bloom.

Nancy Young Levine

ROOM FULL OF MEMORIES

I walk into your vacant room.
A slight fragrance of you remains
haunting the air like an icon
on the pages of my memories.
All your personal possessions are gone,
here where I watched you bloom.

Leafing through chapters, my heart sighs.
What good times we shared along with bad.
I see you there, a charming baby,
then as the pages turn quickly
you're a high school beauty having fun.
I can't stop the tears flowing from my eyes.

Joy and pain stored as souvenirs,
guilt and pleasure mixed together.
If I could only change the print
I'd erase our foolish mistakes.
I lay aside the memory book.
Life consists of laughter and tears.

Parenting has come to an end
and how I lament its passing.
I shall miss sitting on your bed
talking with you in the evening,
rubbing your back and stroking your head—
but you are leaving as my friend.

Judy A. Barnes

1 3

Reflections

THERE ARE THINGS
I WOULD NEVER DO AGAIN

I was thinking yesterday that if I had Motherhood to do over
there are things I would surely do that I did not do the first
time. And there are things I would never do again

I would let Katy talk as much as she wanted while we drove
about town and I tried to remember all my errands
I would not say again in an absent way, *Um-hmmm*
I would really listen to her childish prattle
And not tell her, *Katy, please be quiet*
Now that she lives far away
in Ohio, she's very quiet

And I would stay all night at the hospital with Trella
and not let duties to others surmount her need
for me. I would be with her when nurses
trundled her off to have her tonsils
removed. Now she's in Georgia
and Charles goes with her
to frightening places
and sees that she's
not alone

And I would not let a swimming instructor loosen
Claire's small panic-stricken hands clinging like
pale leeches to the poolside and I would tell
him *I know my child better than you ever*
will and she does not have to go back
into water that threatens to pull
her to its cold deep bottom.
Now that she's a sheriff's
deputy she doesn't need
me to protect her

I would let Polly use the money she earned baby-sitting
to go for cheerleader, sure to make her "popular"
and not tell her she should use her money for
practical things, clothes and lunches, when
what I really wanted was not to drive one
more child to one more activity. Now
that she lives in California, she
doesn't need me to transport
her anywhere

But today, I remember that Polly's letters begin with *Hi, dear one*
and end with *I love you*

I remember when I see the afghan Claire crocheted for me that
   her hands
now are a woman's, capable and strong

I remember Trella telling me when she sees elderly people heavy
with lethargy, she thinks, *My mom has goals*

And I remember when my last visit with Katy ended
she smiled and said, *Come back to see us anytime*

So, if I had Motherhood to do over, there are things I would
   surely do
that I did not do the first time and there are things I would never
do again. But I would read to my children again, and play
with my children again, and work with my children
and hug my children and instill in my children
the knowledge that each one is *Somebody*
again, every time

Barbara Riddle Furr

She was a mother, and a good one, too,
but sometimes she sprinkled words into their oatmeal
so they never knew they were eating Neruda with apples
or Hopkins gravied into stew. Once she stuffed the toes
of their too-big shoes with haiku. She would
fluff alliteration into feather pillows so their
brown heads dreamt onto downy sounds.
She grew allegory in the garden and sautéed
it with mushrooms, baked batches of metonymy
for after-school snacks, and, on their birthdays,
lush similes oozed out from layers of sour-milk chocolate cake.
For special occasions diced sonnets got baked into pies
She tied their sneakers with rhymed couplets
and patched their jeans with woven fibers of heroic verse.
At worse she cursed in spondee and reprimanded
in dactylic tones, but she always tickled with limericks
and tucked worn ballads up under their chins at night.
When a daughter coughed, she made a warm poultice poem
and tied it around the little wheezy chest with a cotton
    dishcloth.
Their hair was braided into villanelle,
washed with frothy verse and evanescent love songs,
patted dry on a strip of formal ode.

Once on a trip an ominous poem came wafting
over the horizon like horsemen of the Apocalypse
till they had to pull off the road and wait for it to blow over.
Most days they got by on license,
and combustible hyperbole poured into the gas tank,
fueled them to soccer.
But when they asked about the workings of the world
she gave only the surety of paradox—
a ewe licking the newborn lamb being eyed by a fox,
crimson song of cardinal on barbed wire,
and a hearty spin on the merry-go-round
of Yeats' widening gyre.

Maureen Tolman Flannery

KNITTING

I

My grandmother's needles
force the soft grey yarn
into patterns old as Europe.
She came from a family of tailors,
and gave each grandchild an afghan
of her own design;
the colors glow like January fire,
the stitches are perfect,
cabled with love.

II

My mother also knits
from patterns and pictures:
mittens with snowflakes
and Fair Isle socks.
Does she weave in June days
of yellow light, the babies
quietly piling blocks, the clean smell
of steam from dampened laundry?

III

My older daughter tries to knit, too,
but her hands can't master the needles,
so she pretends and spends hours
in a tangle of wool and steel.
She is already a maker
of emperor's cloth.
See the fine patterns?
   the royal colors?
   the designs more beautiful than stars?

IV

And here I sit, like a bear in February,
huddled in yards of wool; skeined up in love,
clicking my pen across the page.
I take words and knit them back in poems.
Something could be made of this.

Barbara Crooker

THE GIFT

A special little girl was born early in the morn
in another time and place.
Wanting the very best for her,
knowing I couldn't give enough,
it was the hardest decision I ever made.
In my heart I knew it was my only gift
to one so small,
hoping beyond hope she would understand,
hoping she might forgive.

Christine Ryan Paulus

LOVE LETTERS

HELLO, I AM LOOKING
for a family member I've lost touch with.
Her name was Miriam Goetz and she was born
July 21, 1935. She lived in Cairo, Illinois.
Did you ever call yourself Miriam Goetz,
or do you have information about her?
Please feel free to call me collect.

My former name was Larissa Marie.
I was born in Cairo on April 7, 1956.

I want this woman to know I am
doing well, and would be very happy
if I could meet her and see
how she is doing. Please help me if you can.

LARISSA MARIE, I AM LOOKING
for someone, too—someone who lies in the curve
of yesterday and the seam of tomorrow,
beyond shoal or reef in shivers of the past.

One moment of squall in open sea, one moment
rocked in a still cove, then gone. Now I sing
of seasons lost, of birthdays unmarked,
Valentine hearts without names, and I know
a sun that rises and rises but never sets.

I raised another man's children, Larissa Marie,
felt them ring my waist, saw them steal Mother's Day

violets for my lapel. No, I am not your Miriam,
nor those children's mother. I am their Linda.
I've never been to Illinois but have given birth to
a daughter, so I reach out to you. You wait in

bullrushes for Miriam to offer her kinship as I
wait for Alexandra Rae, born February 14, 1963.
I, too, would like a collect call, a family member
I've lost touch with to say my name.

Susan Terris

MOTHERS AND DAUGHTERS

You—on the beach
patiently lifting
a purple starfish
from a rocky tide pool,
or sitting in the pepper tree,
long hair spilling
over sunlit shoulders.

You, being able to out-talk me
in an argument
nine times out of ten,
being verbally equipped
to launch missiles
against my stronghold,
even when it went against
your own best interests.

Me—holding your oversize
teddy bear
in the upstairs room
after you'd eloped,
and crying—knowing you
would have to live your life
however it led you

Many years later,
Us—on the beach
speaking of the tides in our lives,
the rocky tidepools,
reflecting how grace touches all
and heals and mends,
like a prism, bending us back
to reconstruct
our images.
You and I speak of how
our different lives
have brought us to such
similar conclusions.

Anne Wilson

MOM

My mother embarrassed me so much.
A Gertrude Stein spirit,
she gardened in combat boots, no bra,
and "jeanies" from "Freddies."
She talked to me about tomatoes,
when I didn't want to hear.
Now, I grow tomatoes,
and garden in rafting sandals,
and nylon Nike shorts,
and embarrass my children.

Lois H. Olsen

PASSAGE

Small mouth tender at my breast
Sweet belly heaving while at rest
Our name is Mother-Child.
A little time
A little letting go.

Your walking shoes are broken down
Your tiny tooth rests in a box
Your first smile is in my heart
I watched your world widen with each year
And felt the subtle tug of letting go
Never really knowing what it was.

Playful hours, tearful traumas
Exploring, resisting
Rebelling, insisting
Wide-eyed questions, beguiling antics
Innocent wonder, unlimited hope.
I watched your gradual awakening
Never really knowing
Still letting go.

Your signature (once like mine)
Emerged with its own style
And your voice assumed its own vibration.
You were my pride, my anvil,
My anvil, my pride
And I was yours, too.

Your circle of people expanded
As the world unfolded
Appearing smaller every year.
You were busily designing your
Own place in life.

Then all at once
You were tall and splendid
Your fears could no longer be quelled
By my arms
And you stopped needing my approval.

Glorious transition, perfectly paced
A new dimension to us each
You are the beautiful soul
I have given passage into this world
And now
You are whole.

Dara McLaughlin

We are sitting at lunch when my daughter casually mentions that she and her husband are thinking of "starting a family." "We're taking a survey," she says, half-joking. "Do you think I should have a baby?"

"It will change your life," I say, carefully keeping my tone neutral.

"I know," she says, "no more sleeping in on weekends, no more spontaneous vacations . . ."

But that is not what I meant at all. I look at my daughter, trying to decide what to tell her. I want her to know what she will never learn in childbirth classes. I want to tell her that the physical wounds of childbearing will heal, but that becoming a mother will leave her with an emotional wound so raw that she will forever be vulnerable. I consider warning her that she will never again read a newspaper without asking, "What if that had been MY child?" That every car crash, every house fire, will haunt her. That when she sees pictures of starving children, she will wonder if anything could be worse than watching your child die.

I look at her carefully manicured nails and stylish suit and think that no matter how sophisticated she is, becoming a mother will reduce her to the primitive level of a bear protecting her cub. That an urgent call of "Mom!" will cause her to drop a soufflé or her best crystal without a moment's hesitation. I feel I should warn her that no matter how many years she has invested in her career, she will be professionally derailed by motherhood. She might arrange for childcare, but one day she will be going into an important business meeting and she will think of her baby's sweet smell. She will have to use every ounce of her discipline to keep from running home, just to make sure her baby is all right.

I want my daughter to know that everyday decisions will no longer be routine. That a five-year-old boy's desire to go to the men's room rather than the women's at McDonald's will become a major dilemma. That right there, in the midst of clattering trays and screaming children, issues of independence and gender identity will be weighed against the prospect that a child molester may be lurking in that restroom.

However decisive she may be at the office, she will second-guess herself constantly as a mother. Looking at my attractive daughter, I want to assure her that eventually she will shed the pounds of pregnancy, but she will never feel the same about herself. That her life, now so important, will be of less value to her once she has a child. That she would give it up in a moment to save her offspring, but will also begin to hope for more years—not to accomplish her own dreams, but to watch her child accomplish theirs.

I want her to know that a Caesarian scar or shiny stretch marks will become badges of honor. My daughter's relationship with her husband will change, but not in the way she thinks. I wish she could understand how much more you can love a man who is careful to powder the baby or who never hesitates to play with his child. I think she should know that she will fall in love with him again for reasons she would now find very unromantic.

I wish my daughter could sense the bond she will feel with women throughout history who have tried to stop war, prejudice, and drunk driving. I hope she will understand why I can think rationally about most issues, but become temporarily insane when I discuss the threat of nuclear war to my children's future. I want to describe to my daughter the exhilaration of seeing your child learn to ride a bike. I want to capture for her the belly laugh of a baby who is touching the soft fur of a dog or a cat for the first time. I want her to taste the joy that is so real, it actually hurts.

My daughter's quizzical look makes me realize that tears have formed in my eyes. "You'll never regret it," I finally say. Then I reach across the table, squeeze my daughter's hand and offer a silent prayer for her, and for me, and for all of the mere mortal women who stumble their way into this most wonderful of callings. This blessed gift from God . . . that of being a Mother.

Author unknown

14

Inspiration

She Is the Song, I Am the Music

As I soothe my child to sleep
those words you taught me long ago
come floating through my heart.
Softly I begin to sing
and in the silence of the night
become your instrument again.

Wave Carberry

A Daughter's Song

As you look upon me,
I shall forever see.
As you breathe upon me,
I shall forever breathe.
As we live,
I shall forever love.
As you are within me,
I shall forever be.

Annie Dougherty

MOTHER-DAUGHTER SONG

Our heartbeats, notes
Each separate, but part of the same melody.
The lyrics of our lives
Intertwined,
Composed of love,
Will be sung for generations.

Cheryl Morikawa

FANTASIA

I dream
of giving birth
to
a child
who will ask
'Mother,
what was war?'

Eve Merriam

I HAVE SO MUCH I CAN TEACH HER

I have so much I can teach her and pull out of her. I would say you might encounter defeats but you must never be defeated. I would teach her to love a lot. Laugh a lot at the silliest things and be very serious. I would teach her to love life, I could do that.

Maya Angelou

A BETTER BLESSING

(Rearranging Yeats for My Daughter)

Daughter, the thunder croons
through your night windows and you are
humming. Outside the moon's an enormous
pillow of shine and everywhere her pelvis
rocks you off to sleep. Your eyes are stars.

May strangers, cousins, movie stars, animals
and politicians fall on their face
at your loveliness and Darling,
may all your salads be crazy.
Learn what you choose;
never flourish rooted
like some chaste and hidden tree.

Daughter, I wish your body
safety and strength and strings
for its own song. I wish you long
hair, short hair, shoulder-length
hair, flower crowns (irises,
daisies, chrysanthemums,
violets) and braids. I wish you a green
thumb and an affinity
for beets and spinach. If you ask I will

shutter your windows with amethyst;
I will smash them open for serenades
and rain. I wish you suede,
supple lovers and a preference
for trains. I wish you a mouthful
of prayer, all 8 limbs
of yoga, cellos, rooms strewn
with candles, rosaries, sea
shells and the language
of pomegranates and plums.
I wish you many mothers.

May your eyes be loud
and fragrant and your bones
be naked as fish. And Daughter,
most of all, may you seize
the space of oceans to discover
your singular design.

Sarah Fox

A MOTHER'S DAY GRACE

It's an impossible job
No one can ever do it perfectly
Be willing to accept that there is no success or failure here
Let us give up the burden of unreal expectations
Let us cherish what is and nourish each other's dreams
Let us remember the best and forgive the rest
Allow all the love that may have
slipped into tight places free now
to illuminate the harmony
that always existed
at the very center
of our hearts

Arlene Gay Levine

Author Index

Permissions

GRATEFUL ACKNOWLEDGMENT is made to the authors and publishers for the use of the following material. Every effort has been made to contact original sources. If notified, the publishers will be pleased to rectify an omission in future editions.

Kim Addonizio for "Gravity."
Martha K. Baker for "The Cat's Meow."
Judy A. Barnes for "Room Full of Memories."
Ellen Bass for "There Are Times in Life When One Does the Right Thing."
Gail McCoig Blanton for "Wedding Farewell."
Gayle Brandeis for "Brit Ha-Hayim."
Regina Murray Brault for "Mother Tongue."
Danielle Brigante for "Strength."
Kathryn Byron for "Through the Eyes of Her Child."
Rosalie Calabrese for "Baby Steps."
Wave Carberry for "She Is the Song, I Am the Music."
Kelly Cherry for "Becoming My Mother" and "The Conversation."
Madonna Dries Christensen for "Prom Night."
Elayne Clift for "When Did I Weep?"
SuzAnne C. Cole for "To My Daughter, Wearing Her Father's Shoes."
Kathy Conde for "I Take Your *Yes!* and Echo It Back."
Barbara Crooker for "Family Sampler," "Knitting," "Me 'n' Bruce Springsteen Take My Baby Off to College," "My Middle Daughter, on the Edge of Adolescence, Learns to Play the Saxophone," "Recipe for Grief," "Rites of Passage," "Separation," and "Tideline."

Mary Maude Daniels for "Growing Daughter."

Mona Davis for "The Most Beautiful Lily in Heaven."

Corrine De Winter for "Waiting to Heal."

Annie Dougherty for "A Daughter's Song."

Mary Eastham for "A Promise to My Sick Child."

Elizabeth B. Estes for "Grandbaby."

Alice Evans for "Grandmother's Power."

Maureen Tolman Flannery for "Bond," "First Daughter," "Involuntary
Craftsmanship," "Learning to Read," "Mothered on Poems," "Newborn," and
"Suitable Occupations for Mothers of Adolescents."

Sarah Fox for "A Better Blessing" and "Taking a Nap."

Susan Fridkin for "Grandmother's Gifts" and "The Naming."

Barbara Riddle Furr for "There Are Things I Would Never Do Again."

Ingrid Goff-Maidoff for "How Might I Entice You to Be Born?"

June Cotner Graves for "One of the Hardest Things."

Maryanne Hannan for "Viaticum for a Young Daughter."

Peggy Hong for "The Five-Year Change" and "The Growing Into."

Margaret Anne Huffman for "Birth Pangs Redux," "Dancing Partners," and
"Heart's Child: In Honor of My Adopted Daughter."

Christina Keenan for "Sometimes."

Kim Konopka for "Small Offerings."

Susan Landon for "The Courage to Be."

Pamela L. Laskin for "Wait."

Arlene Gay Levine for "A Mother's Day Grace" and "In Retrospect."

Nancy Young Levine for "Pink Pearls."

Diane Sher Lutovich for "Visitor."

Jill Noblit MacGregor for "Birth Rights" and "The Conception."

Katharyn Howd Machan for "My Daughter, Ten, Dresses As an Alien."

Arlene L. Mandell for "Little Girl Grown."

Marguerite McKirgan for "Time Warp."

Dara McLaughlin for "Passage."

Meadow Geese Press for "Parents' Day on Campus" from *Coasts: Collected Poems Bound by the Sea* by Mary Kennan Herbert. Copyright © 2000 by Mary Kennan Herbert. Reprinted by kind permission of Meadow Geese Press.

Maude Meehan for "Cartographer," "Continuum," "Heritage," "New Game Song," "New Life," and "Waiting."

Ann E. Michael for "To My Daughter."

Honor Moore for "Ladies and Gentlemen," excerpted from *Mourning Pictures* from *The New Women's Theatre,* edited by Honor Moore. Copyright © 1977 by Honor Moore. Reprinted by kind permission of the author.

Cheryl Morikawa for "Beyond Words" and "Mother-Daughter Song."

Andrea O'Brien for "Consecration."

Sheila O'Connor for "Gifts," "I Will Write About You As a Mystery," and "Morning Vows."

Lois H. Olsen for "Mom."

Joan Shea O'Neal for "Initiation."

Stephanie B. Palladino for "Saying Good-bye."

Thelma J. Palmer for "Note of Advice to the Good Nurse, Death."

Christine Ryan Paulus for "The Gift."

Nita Penfold for "As I Watch My Daughter Marry."

Andrea Potos for "Nursing," "Pregnant Love," and "With Child."

Marian Reiner for "Fantasia" from *A Sky Full of Poems* by Eve Merriam. Copyright © 1964, 1970, 1973 by Eve Merriam. Used by permission of Marian Reiner.

Linda Goodman Robiner for "African Violets."

Daniel Roselle for "A Father's View of Mother and Daughter."

Jane Butkin Roth for "I Should Be So Lucky" and "The Way She Greets the Day."

Ellen Sherck for "A Wish of Mine."

Jennifer Shunfenthal for "I Hate Broccoli" and "My Mother Is the Best."

Sherri Waas Shunfenthal for "Daughter," "Loving Hands," and "Side by Side."

Lois Greene Stone for "Everything Leaves Traces" and "Unchanged."

Susan Terris for "Love Letters."

B. G. Thurston for "Placenta Previa."

Donna Wahlert for "Attending the Birth of My Granddaughter," "Before My Granddaughter's Surgery," and "Sacrament."

Joanna M. Weston for "A Child's Surgery."

Anne Wilson for "Mothers and Daughters."

Barbara Younger for "A Note to My Husband's Mother."

Permissions compiled by Rebecca Pirtle.

Grateful acknowledgment is given to the following individuals for the photographs that appear in this book.

"Pregnancy": Sarah Beckett, © Donald Beckett; "Birth": June Cotner Graves and Kirsten Myrvang, from the author's private collection; "Babyhood": Gretchen Weiher and Sana Weiher Keller, © Paul Keller; "Toddlerhood": Cheryl Edmonson and Christa E. Edmonson, © Chuck Edmonson: "Childhood": Amber Berard and Shirley Concotilli, © Corrine De Winter; "Adolescence": Sandi and Kari Van Ausdal, from their private collection; "Leaving Home": June Cotner Graves and Kirsten Myrvang, from the author's private collection; "Adulthood": Marina Alonso and Agueda B. Chevin, © Sandi Van Ausdal; "Grandmotherhood": Betty E. Morikawa, Chelsea E. Lye, and Christa E. Edmonson, © Ronald K. Morikawa; "Later Years": Hannah Lahnala holding Rebecca Pirtle, © Hal Bush; "Illness": Eveline Baxter, Kirsten Myrvang, and June Cotner Graves, from the author's private collection; "Partings": June Cotner Graves and daughter Kirsten Myrvang at her mother's grave, from the author's private collection; "Reflections": Dorothy A. (Brewer) Bush, Rebecca L. (Bush) Pirtle; Hannah Lahnala, Dorothy F. (Lahnala) Brewer, © Hal Bush; "Inspiration": photo taken on the beach in St. Sebastian, Spain, © Adrienne Campbell-Holt.

About the Author

A bestselling author, anthologist, speaker, and consultant, JUNE COTNER's books include *Mothers and Daughters* (published by Random House); *Graces, Bedside Prayers, Get Well Wishes,* and *Animal Blessings* (all published by HarperCollins San Francisco); *Bless the Day* (published by Kodansha); *Family Celebrations* and *Heal Your Soul, Heal the World* (both published by Andrews McMeel); and *The Home Design Handbook* (published by Henry Holt and Company). She has three forthcoming anthologies. June has appeared on national radio programs and her books have been featured in many national publications, including *USA Today, Better Homes & Gardens, Woman's Day,* and *Family Circle.*

June has taught workshops and given presentations at bookstores throughout the country and the Pacific Northwest Writer's Association Conference, the Pacific Northwest Booksellers Association Conference, and The Learning Annex in New York, San Francisco, Los Angeles, and San Diego. With her consulting business, Book Proposal Services, June shares her knowledge of writing strong and successful book proposals. With her second business, Book Marketing Services, June helps authors market their books successfully. For information on scheduling June as a speaker or for consultation requests, you may contact June at one of the addresses listed below.

A graduate of the University of California at Berkeley, June has an impressive background of twenty-five years in marketing. She is the mother of two grown children and lives in Poulsbo, Washington (a small town outside of Seattle), with her husband, two dogs, and two cats. Her hobbies include yoga, hiking, backpacking, cross-country skiing, and gardening.

For more information, you may access June's website at www.junecotner.com (email: june@junecotner.com) or write to her at: June Cotner, P.O. Box 2765, Poulsbo, Washington 98370.